For Guillaume
M·E·
For Stewart
G·R·

First American edition published in 1995 by
Crocodile Books, USA
An imprint of Interlink Publishing Group, Inc.
99 Seventh Avenue, Brooklyn, New York 11215
Text © by Mark Ezra 1995
Illustrations © by Gavin Rowe 1995
Published simultaneously in Great Britain by Magi Publications

Library of Congress Cataloging-in-Publication Data

Ezra, Mark,
     The prickly hedgehog/Mark Ezra; pictures by Gavin Rowe.
        p. cm.
     Summary: Little Hedgehog's legs are too short for him to keep up
with his family on their trip to the country.
     ISBN 1-56656-189-2 (hardback)
     (1. Hedgehogs—Fiction, 2. Lost children—Fiction.) I. Rowe,
Gavin, Ill. II. Title.
PZ7.E987Pr 1995
[E]—dc20

94-48116

CIP
AC

Printed and bound in Belgium
10 9 8 7 6 5 4 3 2 1

MARK EZRA

The Prickly Hedgehog

pictures by GAVIN ROWE

Crocodile Books, USA

An imprint of Interlink Publishing Group, Inc.
NEW YORK

It was Little Hedgehog's first time out.
His mother was leading a food hunt,
and he hurried along behind his four prickly
brothers and sisters as fast as his short legs
could carry him. But it was no good.
Before long, he was left way behind.

A big butterfly landed on Little Hedgehog's
snout. He tried to brush it off, but it fluttered
away over his head and he fell backwards.
By the time he had picked himself up,
his family had completely disappeared.

They can't be too far, thought
Little Hedgehog, pulling off all the
dry leaves that were stuck to his coat.

Oh good, there they were in the clearing ahead!
Little Hedgehog grunted with joy.
He scuttled forward, but all he
found was —

a circle of hedgehog mushrooms
with little spines poking out from
under their caps.
"Mm, these look good to eat," he said,
as he stuck four of them on his back.
"But where *is* my family?" he wondered sadly.

Ah, there they were, at the foot
of that hedge! Little Hedgehog's
eyes lit up, and his heart beat faster.
But when he got there, all he found
was a broken teasel twig with some
teasels on it.

"Wrong again!" said Little Hedgehog. He ran
on and bumped into the trunk of a big tree.
"How tall it is!" he said, looking upwards.
"But what's that up there?"

Little Hedgehog thought
he saw his family high up on a
branch. It seemed an awfully long
way to climb, but some ivy grew up
the tree, and he was able to find
a foothold.

Twig by twig and branch by branch
he climbed up through the leaves.
He teetered along a thin bough
toward the spiny little group.
He had never been so scared in
his life, but he was very brave
and didn't look down.

When he reached the
end of the branch,
Little Hedgehog saw that
his climb was in vain.
"Stupid me!" he exclaimed
—for it was only a bunch
of spiny chestnuts.

He reached out and stuck four of
them on his back. But it wasn't easy,
and when he turned around, he lost his
balance and fell.

As he fell down and down,
he curled into a tight ball—
and bounced onto a soft bed
of leaves.
"Bother!" said Little Hedgehog,
wriggling round to pull the
leaves from his spiny back.

Suddenly Little Hedgehog heard a loud
noise, and a huge creature bounced
up to him. He didn't know this was a
friendly dog, and he was terrified.
Once again, he curled right up into a
tight ball to protect himself.

Moments passed.
Had the creature gone?
Little Hedgehog uncurled,
and just then he saw the dog's
big head bending down
towards him . . . .

The dog picked him up in his powerful jaws
and trotted along the path.
Then, suddenly, the dog dropped him on a
soft mossy bank.

Little Hedgehog stayed curled
up for a long time.
He was still very frightened.
Then he heard some familiar
snorting sounds.
He opened his eyes . . . .

And there were his mother,
his brothers, and his sisters!
"Where have you been?"
asked his mother.

Little Hedgehog uncurled
himself.
"Oh, just hunting for food,"
he said. "See what I've brought
back for you!"

His mother looked at the feast of food
on Little Hedgehog's back.
"Mushrooms and chestnuts!" cried all his
brothers and sisters, and they ate until
their tummies were full. Then they fell
asleep under their favorite hedge.

Little Hedgehog's mother licked his face
clean and found him some ripe berries.
The prickly little hedgehog never told his
mother all about his adventures, but I think
she must have guessed.
Don't you?